HENRY WINKLER
BORN ACTOR

Library of Congress Cataloging in Publication Data

Jacobs, Linda.
    Henry Winkler, born actor.

    (Headliners I)
    SUMMARY: A biography of Henry Winkler whose rise to
television stardom fulfilled a childhood dream to become an
actor.
    1. Winkler, Henry, 1945-   — Juvenile
literature. 2. Actors — United States — Biography — Juvenile
literature. [1. Winkler, Henry, 1945-   2. Actors and
actresses] I. Title. II. Series.
PN2287.W497J3   792'.028'0924   [B] [92] 77-27991
ISBN 0-88436-426-7 lib. bdg.
ISBN 0-88436-427-5 pbk.

Published 1978. Produced by EMC Corporation
180 East Sixth Street, Saint Paul, Minnesota 55101
Printed in the United States of America
0 9 8 7 6 5 4 3 2 1

HENRY WINKLER
BORN ACTOR

BY LINDA JACOBS

EMC CORPORATION ST. PAUL, MINNESOTA

"It may sound dumb," Henry Winkler says, "But I think people were born to do certain things. I was born to be an actor."

He's felt that way for a long time. It started when he was only eight years old. He remembers a movie called *Rear Window*. It starred Jimmy Stewart. For most people, it was just a good movie with a favorite star.

For Henry, it was magic. It opened dreams of a whole new world. As an actor he could create living people. He could become those people for a time. He could do other things. He could think other thoughts and feel other feelings.

"There was nothing I wanted more," Henry says.

Today he has his dream. It's turned out to be bigger than even he imagined. He's not just another actor. He's a superstar. He hasn't created just another character. He's built a living legend.

The legend is Fonzie. The Fonze. Super cool. Biker. Semi-tough of the fifties.

Fonzie is a rebel in a world where everybody tries to be like everybody else. He's not mean, though. He's just honest. He's himself. If people like him that way, fine. If they don't, also fine.

He was born to be an actor.

"Fonzie is totally confident," Henry says. "He may be the last honest man."

These qualities have made Fonzie a folk hero. Henry enjoys that. He is glad that the character he created is so popular. He is grateful to the fans. He is grateful to Fonzie for making him a star.

But there are problems in being Arthur Fonzarelli, Jr. Though Henry created Fonzie out of his own fantasy, he is not really a carefree biker, always ready with wisecracks. He is a quiet and sensitive young man. He is a serious actor. He wants people to recognize his talents. He wants challenges in his work. He's afraid that Fonzie could become a trap. The public might not accept him in other roles. He is afraid of being what movie people called "typed."

If that happened, people wouldn't ever accept him in other roles. He would be playing the Fonze—or someone like him—for the rest of his career.

"I struggled too hard to become an actor to end up like that," Henry says.

He did struggle hard. But not in the usual way. Henry never pounded pavements. He was never out of work for long stretches of time. His problems started long before that. They started with his family.

Harry and Ilse Winkler were well-educated people. They had been well-to-do in Germany. Then came the government of Adolph Hitler. As Jews, the Winklers had to leave their home. They came to America. They settled in New York City. And they started over.

At first Henry felt more at home on Broadway than in Hollywood.

Mr. Winkler became head of a large lumber company, doing business all over the world. Both he and his wife liked the finer things in life. Good literature. Good music. Good art. Most of all, good education.

They wanted their children to grow up to like these things, too. Their oldest, Beatrice, was no problem. She took well to the life they wanted. When Henry was born on October 30, 1945, his parents thought he would be the same way.

Mr. Winkler knew what he wanted for his son. He would get the best possible education. He would do well in school. He would win honors in college.

When he was grown up, he would be a diplomat. That had been Mr. Winkler's own secret dream. He had never been able to do it. Now he had a son to carry on.

Of course, Henry didn't know about those plans when he was little. He only knew that he was important to his family. In fact, he was a little bit spoiled. His mother and father made him feel special. So did his sister. Everybody loved Henry. His world was safe and happy. No problems. No hurts. No worries.

It was such a safe world that starting school became a problem. Henry had never played with many children. He had never rough-and-tumbled. The other children in his class looked like fearsome enemies to him.

His life became harder at home, too. His parents started to push. They wanted him to start out well in school. They wanted him to take an interest in his studies.

Unfortunately, Henry couldn't work up the kind of interest they wanted. Their worry, along with his problems with other children, made his world into a painful one.

He was a sensitive boy. He was a daydreamer. At home, he was told to stop all that and become a good student. At school, on the playground, he was told to stop all that and become a regular guy. The other kids teased him.

Henry took it all to heart. He felt pulled apart. He felt like a failure. He couldn't give his parents what they wanted. And he couldn't give the kids what they wanted.

Sometimes it all got so painful that Henry thought about killing himself. That would show people. He would imagine everybody crying at his funeral. They'd tell each other how mean they had been. They'd tell each other what a wonderful boy Henry had been. They'd be sorry.

Henry's ideas of suicide were only daydreams. He was raised in a strong Jewish tradition. Jews are taught respect for life. Henry wasn't serious. His thoughts didn't show a sick personality. They did show a boy with a lot of imagination.

It was that same imagination that made him want to be an actor. When he came home from seeing *Rear Window* he was glowing with his brand new dream. He told his parents about it.

"No son of mine is going to be an actor," Harry Winkler said. Henry would be a diplomat. Or at least a prominent businessman. That was that.

"Don't worry," Mrs. Winkler told her husband. "It's just a child's fancy. He'll forget it in a week."

But Henry didn't forget. He became more determined as he grew older. He practiced being other people. He stood in front of his mirror and tried to show different feelings. He started mouthing the words to his favorite records. He couldn't sing at all. But he had a natural dancer's grace. He moved to the music. He pretended to hold a microphone. He put emotion into his "songs." He looked like a real rock star.

As Henry's interest in acting grew stronger, his grades grew weaker. Mr. and Mrs. Winkler got upset. It might be all right for a child to have a crazy dream. He'd grow out of it. But it was not all right when the dream hurt his schoolwork.

Henry and his father began to have arguments. Loud ones. Mr. Winkler sounded harsh. That's how Henry saw him at the time. Downright mean. Now he realizes that his father was scared. He saw his son coming to "no good." He saw his dream for Henry's future wrecked. He had worked too long and hard to take that lightly.

When Henry finished elementary school, his parents took firm action. He wouldn't go on in public schools. He would go to an exclusive private school. There, they would get him ready for college. Maybe they could even make him like to study.

Henry protested. But it didn't help. He was enrolled in McBurney's School for Boys. It was near his home. He was at least glad of that. Boarding school would have been terrible.

McBurney's put pressure on Henry. The boys there were more serious than they had been in public school. They didn't pick on him as much. They were all college bound. They all had to work hard to keep their grades up.

Henry was glad that they didn't tease as much. But they caused him another problem. They made him feel stupid. They didn't have to say or do anything to him. They just had to be themselves. They just had to do their usual top schoolwork. Henry couldn't keep up.

Henry believes in Fonzie's honesty. He hopes audiences will accept him in other roles too.

"I always got the lowest grades in my class," he says.

Those low grades got him in trouble at home, as usual. They also kept him out of many of the school plays. At McBurney's, grades had to be up for a student to be in outside activities. Drama was an extra activity. That left Henry out much of the time.

When he did manage to get in a play, he had another problem. The Headmaster at McBurney's, was also the drama coach. He didn't like being drama coach. Sometimes, he would take it out on the boys. He'd put them down. He'd point out even the smallest mistakes. And he would do it in front of everybody.

He was extra hard on Henry. He didn't like Henry's attitude toward schoolwork. He didn't like the way Henry cared so much about being in the plays. He was like Mr. Winkler. He thought boys should be interested in more "serious" matters.

"You don't have any talent," he told Henry once. "You'll never be an actor."

Henry didn't like him. He didn't want to believe him. But he didn't have a lot of self-confidence either. The criticism hurt. Henry wondered if his big dream really was stupid. Maybe he didn't have any talent. He knew for sure that he wasn't movie-star handsome.

All those things discouraged him. They made him doubt. But they couldn't make him give up. The dream was too important to him. He couldn't shake it. He couldn't stop believing that he was born to be an actor.

Henry Winkler enjoys children. He once thought of child psychology as a back up for his acting.

He did try to get interested in something else. For a while, he worked with underprivileged kids. He volunteered his time. He taught them games. He listened to their problems. That made him feel good. He enjoyed the work. It even made his family happy.

"Maybe Henry is getting over this acting thing," they told each other.

But Henry wasn't. And when his folks found out, his father started yelling again. The fights seemed worse than ever. Mrs. Winkler at least didn't yell. She showed her feelings in other ways. But she showed them.

"She served it with breakfast," Henry says, "Bacon, eggs and guilt."

The Winklers loved their son. They weren't really mean to him. But they simply could not understand his dream. They were desperate.

When Henry graduated from high school, they made one try. He would go to college. They would pay his expenses. He could be involved in drama. But he would have to study something else, too. Anything else.

Henry remembered how he had enjoyed his work with underprivileged kids. If he couldn't make it as an actor, maybe he could help children. That would be a good life. It was also wise to have something else in mind. Even if he wouldn't give up acting, acting might give *him* up. He might not be able to have the kind of career he wanted.

"It's just a backup," he told himself, when he decided to study child psychology.

The Fonzie t-shirt in the first row tells how popular the character has become.

His parents were thrilled at that decision. If their son wouldn't be a diplomat or a businessman, maybe he would be a psychologist. They had high hopes as young Henry went off to Emerson College.

Henry watches an "aaaaay" from the thumbs of a very young fan.

As usual, Henry himself had other ideas. He did study psychology. But it was only the backup he had meant it to be. He started right off in drama.

He was good. He did many plays at Emerson. Everyone there thought he had the talent to be an actor. He got so much praise that even his parents started to notice. They still didn't like the idea. But they did go to see Henry in some of his plays.

Once, when he was doing *Carousel*, his mother had a long talk with the drama coach.

"Do you think Henry really has talent?" she asked.

The coach didn't even stop to think. Yes, Henry had talent. He had the ability to make it as an actor. But he would need something besides ability. He would need luck.

It hurt Mrs. Winkler to hear that. She never had much faith in luck. To her and her husband, success was a matter of education and hard work. Nobody could depend on luck.

Still, she saw Henry's joy in acting. She started to believe in his talent. If he had to be an actor, she hoped that he would find his luck.

Henry enjoyed the company of Laverne and Shirley.

"He must do what he feels is right," she told her husband.

Mr. Winkler didn't like to hear that one bit. But he did stop yelling as much as before.

Things were beginning to work out for Henry's dream. He learned a lot about acting at Emerson. He learned a lot about life, too.

His college acting success gave him more confidence. He was a somebody. He didn't have to feel bad around people who made better grades. He liked himself better so he liked others better, too. He joined a fraternity. He went to parties and dances. He was happier than he'd ever been in his life.

At least he was until his senior year. Then everything fell apart inside him. College life wasn't to blame. It was the same. Henry was becoming different.

He suddenly realized that he wasn't an eight-year-old, seeing a good movie and starting a dream. He wasn't a high school boy, arguing with his drama coach. He was about to graduate from college. He was a man.

That meant a man's responsibilities. And a man's hard questions about his own future. Maybe he had the talent to be an actor. He knew he had the drive. But would he have the luck? Could he really make it? It had been one thing to dream of acting. It was quite another to plan for it as a job.

"For the first time in my life, I wondered if that's what I really wanted," he says. He had known doubts before, of course. But they had been about whether or not he could succeed as an actor. They were never about whether or not he wanted to try.

That last year of college was a hard time for Henry. Of course, he did decide to go ahead with acting. But this time, it was the hard decision of a man. It wasn't the dream of a boy any longer.

"I came to the point that I was ready to pay the price," he says.

With that new and realistic goal, Henry finally convinced his parents. They gave up worrying about him being an actor. They had watched him in college. They had seen him turn a crazy dream into a serious plan. If he wanted to be an actor that badly, then they would go along. They would hope with him. They would help him all they could.

"If you're going to be an actor, be a good one," Mr. Winkler said. "Get your Master's Degree in theater."

Henry almost had to laugh. His folks had changed a little. They had given in to his ambition. But to them, education would always be the answer to everything. Maybe, he thought, they were right.

He didn't want to be just a "personality." He wanted to be a serious actor. In fact, he knew that being serious and well-trained was his only hope. He wasn't a glamor boy. He never would be. He was only average looking. He was short. No theatrical agent was going to run up to him on the street and beg him to play a romantic lead in a big new movie.

If he was going to have a chance, he'd have to be better than good. He'd have to be almost perfect. For once, he had to agree with his dad. Education was the answer.

He entered Yale School of Drama as a graduate student. At last he felt fully alive. The doubts of his senior year were almost gone. He had a new confidence that he would make it. No matter what.

The years at Yale were among the happiest in Henry's life. He kept up the growth he started at Emerson; as an actor and as a person. He had good roles in important plays. People admired his work. Other drama students talked about how they wished they could be "as good as Henry." The teachers used him as an example of talent and hard work.

To add icing to the cake, his parents became his greatest fans. They had already accepted that Henry was serious. Now they went a step further. They were proud of him. They respected his ability at last.

That made Henry feel good. So did other things at that time in his life. He was more relaxed about himself. Being at Yale made him feel like a real actor. He wasn't someone just dreaming of being an actor. Because of that, he could cut loose and enjoy other things, too. At Emerson, he had started to be more social. He had learned to let himself have fun for it's own sake. At Yale, he became even more open to new experiences.

For a year, he lived in a big old house with six other people. Men and women. Each person had his or her own room. Each had a separate life. But they shared, too. They were like a big family. It was like living with a house full of brothers and sisters.

Henry with his sister and parents.

Henry liked the casual happiness of that life. He enjoyed the chance to be close to people who weren't actors. All of the others were graduate students. But not in drama. Henry was the only actor. Often, he would entertain his friends in the evening. He would do skits for them. He would get everybody dancing. Sometimes, he would grab part of the vacuum cleaner for a "microphone" and do his old rock singing routine. The other guys would grab other parts of the cleaner for musical "instruments" and back him up.

Henry introduced young viewers to Shakespeare in "Henry Winkler meets William Shakespeare."

"There were really some fun times back then," Henry says. "Some special times."

When those times came to an end, Henry again felt at loose ends. This time, though, he wasn't as frightened as before. He had earned his Master's Degree in his chosen field. He had proven his ability in the academic world of drama. Now it was time to start proving it in the professional world.

The only question was how and where to make that start. Henry didn't have to wait long for his answer. The people in the Yale Drama Department had liked him so well that they asked him to try for the Yale Repertory Company. He did. And he was accepted right away.

The Yale Repertory Company is a professional group. Their actors all learn several plays. They might put on Shakespeare one night and a modern comedy the next. It was great experience. It paid fairly well. Henry had his first professional job as an actor.

He stayed with the Company for a year and a half. He enjoyed the varied work. It gave him a chance to test himself as an actor. He also enjoyed making his own living. He was independent. He could pay his own way. And he was doing it all in the field he had chosen.

After a time, though, Henry knew that he would have to grow even more. He would have to strike out for new challenges as an actor. He tried his luck in off-Broadway plays. He got some good reviews for his work. He got an agent and began finding work in television commercials. Soon, he was making enough money so that even his family had to call him a total success.

Henry's role as the Fonze is very different from Shakespeare.

Henry was perhaps the only one who didn't call himself a success. Commercials and off-Broadway plays were fine for a start. But they wouldn't do for an entire career. He wanted more and bigger parts.

During that period, his old self-doubts began to return. They had never completely left him. Success had simply pushed them into the background. Now he wondered if this would be as far as it went. The idea made him feel sick. He wanted to do so much. He wanted to be so much. All he needed was a chance.

The chance came when he was cast in his first movie. It was a low-budget picture called *Lords of Flatbush*. The story was about gang members in the fifties. Henry got his first D.A. haircut. He wore his first black leather jacket. In a sense, he was Fonzie before Fonzie ever existed.

Lords of Flatbush made a lot of money at the box office. It got good reviews. Several of the reviews said great things about Henry. He was thrilled. In his excitement, he couldn't resist doing something he had dreamed about for a long time. He carefully cut out one of the best reviews. He underlined the parts that talked about his great performance. Then he put it into an envelope and mailed it—to the drama coach at McBurney's School for Boys.

"Maybe it was a dumb thing to do," Henry says now, "but it made me feel good."

After the movie, Henry's agent hit him with another big decision. She thought he had done all he could in New York. He had a good list of credits. He had shown himself to be a solid professional. It was time to try his luck in Hollywood.

Henry didn't like the idea. But he knew that his agent was right. It was time. It would be hard, leaving home and friends and family. It would be scary at first. But it had to be done.

Luckily, Henry had saved some money. He took it all and flew to Los Angeles. He hated the city right away. It was big and spread out. It was casual and easygoing. People in Los Angeles talked about movies and surfing. In New York, people talked about books and classical music.

Within a week, Henry wondered if he had made an awful mistake. In another week, he knew he hadn't made a mistake at all. He got his first part. It was on the "Mary Tyler Moore Show." Other parts followed soon after that.

"I was never out of work for more than a few days," Henry says.

He had only been in Hollywood for a couple of months when he was asked to read for a small part. It was a new character that the producers were putting into a show called "Happy Days." The character was, of course, Arthur Fonzarelli, Jr. He had not been in the pilot of the show. But the producers thought he would be interesting for the viewers.

Henry takes his role as Fonzie seriously.

Henry went to read. While he was waiting his turn, he got scared. The other actors all looked big and tough. They looked like they could really be tough guys from the fifties.

"There I was, a short Jewish kid with a big nose," Henry says.

The leather jacket was Henry's own idea.

Henry talked to the producers. He read for them. But he didn't expect anything to come of it.

A few days later, he got the call that was to change his life. He was to play Fonzie. Of course, Henry had no idea at the time how important his role would be. He only had six lines in the first show he did.

He took those six lines seriously. He took Fonzie seriously, too. The script first called for him to wear a cloth jacket and loafers. Henry thought back to the *Lords of Flatbush*. Why couldn't Fonzie wear a black leather jacket and motorcycle boots?

Okay, the producers said. That sounded like a good idea. They would try it.

Of course, everybody knows now that it worked.

Fonzie caught on so well that the character had to grow. He had more lines. In time, Henry Winkler earned billing as one of the stars of the show.

As Fonzie became a legend, Henry has found his own life changed. He had gotten used to being respected as an actor. But he had never known the kind of attention that the Fonze brought him. Fans mobbed him in the street. They pushed each other just to get his autograph or maybe just to touch him.

Roz Kelly played Fonzie's special girlfriend, Pinky.

People in Hollywood say that Henry has kept his head. He hasn't gotten phony. He hasn't gotten a "big head." He hasn't even gone out and spent a whole lot of money.

He bought himself a house and an Audi car. He bought himself a really good new stereo. He likes to have good clothes. But he doesn't want to live like a millionaire. He wants a quiet life. He wants a chance to grow even more as an actor.

His family is now solidly behind him. His mother has become his biggest fan. She tells all her friends about what Henry is doing. She invites them over to watch the show with her.

"She never misses 'Happy Days,' " Henry says. That makes him proud.

Many things about his life these days make him proud. But underneath that pride, there is also fear.

"I want people to know that I'm not Fonzie," Henry says.

He knows the dangers of becoming forever tied to the character he has created. He intends to keep away from those dangers.

He is already planning what to do when the series ends. Those plans do not include playing more parts like Fonzie. He wants to branch out.

His next big goal is success in movies. He wants important parts in important pictures. He wants to do the kind of thing that gets noticed for Academy Awards.

"I have already written a dozen acceptance speeches," Henry says. He grins. He knows that, so far, the idea of an "Oscar" is only a dream. It's as much of a dream as that first idea of becoming an actor at all. When he was young, nobody thought he'd get that one, either.

"Happy Days" star Marion Ross .

People around the world are fans of Fonzie. Here he greets Janelle Commissong, Miss Universe.

Today, some people doubt that he will get his newest dream. Movie success is hard to come by these days. It is for the few—and the lucky. Henry himself doubts sometimes. He is still bothered by the old self-doubt. But bothered or not, he will try. He will read movie scripts. He will pick roles he cares about. He will do his best. And he will hope that the public will accept him without Fonzie.

"There's nothing else I can do," he says softly. "It's simple. I was born to be an actor."

Fonzie has gone from having six lines to star billing on "Happy Days."

PHOTO CREDITS